TIMELINE OF JACKSON POLLOCK'S LIFE

1912 Paul Jackson Pollock is born in Cody, Wyoming.

1913 -1917 The Pollock family moves around while Jackson's dad looks for work. They finally settle in California.

1927 Jackson works on a surveying crew at the Grand Canyon with his Dad and his brother Sande.

1928 Jackson moves to Los Angeles and goes to high school there. An art teacher there introduces him to modern abstract art.

1930 Jackson travels with his older brother, Charles, to New York City. He begins taking classes at the Art Students League.

1935 Jackson is hired to paint murals as part of a U.S. government program.

1939 Jackson sees Pablo Picasso's painting *Guernica*. He is amazed by it, and returns often to make sketches of this powerful work of art.

THIS WAY

UP HERE

1941 Jackson is excited to have one of his paintings exhibited alongside works by Pablo Picasso, Henri Matisse, Stuart Davis, and Lee Krasner.

1943 Jackson has his first one-man show. The Museum of Modern Art buys one of his paintings!

1945 Jackson and Lee Krasner get married. They leave New York City and buy a farmhouse on Long Island.

1946 Jackson begins his famous action paintings.

1947 -1953 Jackson becomes super-famous. *Life* magazine features Jackson in a big story.

1955 Even though Jackson Pollock is known all over the world for his amazing paintings, he is often depressed. He pretty much stops painting.

1956 Jackson Pollock is killed in a car accident on Long Island.

GETTING TO KNOW THE WORLD'S GREATEST ARTISTS

JACKSON POLLOCK

WRITTEN AND ILLUSTRATED BY MIKE VENEZIA

CONSULTANT MEG MOSS

CHILDREN'S PRESS®

An Imprint of Scholastic Inc.

*For the many future great artists and authors at
P.S. 111 in Manhattan. Keep up the good work!*

Cover photo: *Number 34, 1949*, 1949. Enamel on paper mounted on masonite. 22 x 30-1/2 in.
© Edward W. Root Bequest. 57.206/Munson-Williams-Proctor Arts Institute/Art Resource, NY/
© 2016 The Pollock-Krasner Foundation/Artists Rights Society (ARS), New York.

Library of Congress Cataloging-in-Publication Data

Names: Venezia, Mike, author.
Title: Jackson Pollock / written and illustrated by Mike Venezia.
Description: Revised edition. | New York, NY : Children's Press, an Imprint
  of Scholastic Inc., 2017. | Series: Getting to know the world's greatest
  artists | Includes bibliographical references and index.
Identifiers: LCCN 2016022633| ISBN 9780531221914 (library binding :
  alk. paper) | ISBN 9780531220894 (paperback : alk. paper)
Subjects: LCSH: Pollock, Jackson, 1912-1956—Juvenile literature. |
  Painters—United States—Biography—Juvenile literature. | Abstract
  expressionism—United States—Juvenile literature.
Classification: LCC ND237.P73 V46 2017 | DDC 759.13 [B] —dc23
LC record available at https://lccn.loc.gov/2016022633

1 2 3 4 5 6 7 8 9 10 R 26 25 24 23 22 21 20 19 18 17

Jackson Pollock was born in Cody, Wyoming, in 1912. He was the youngest of five brothers, and grew up to be one of the greatest artists of the twentieth century.

Galaxy, by Jackson Pollock. 1947. Oil and aluminum paint on canvas, 43 ½ x 34 inches. Joslyn Art Museum, Omaha, Nebraska. Gift of Miss Peggy Guggenheim. © 1994 The Pollock-Krasner Foundation/ARS, New York.

Jackson is best known for the huge paintings he made by splattering, throwing, and dripping paint onto his canvases.

Jackson used old, hardened
brushes, sticks, and anything else he
could find that would splatter on
paint the way he liked.

Jackson's style of art is often called Abstract Expressionism. Because Jackson moved around a lot and used so much energy while he painted, he preferred to call his style Action Painting.

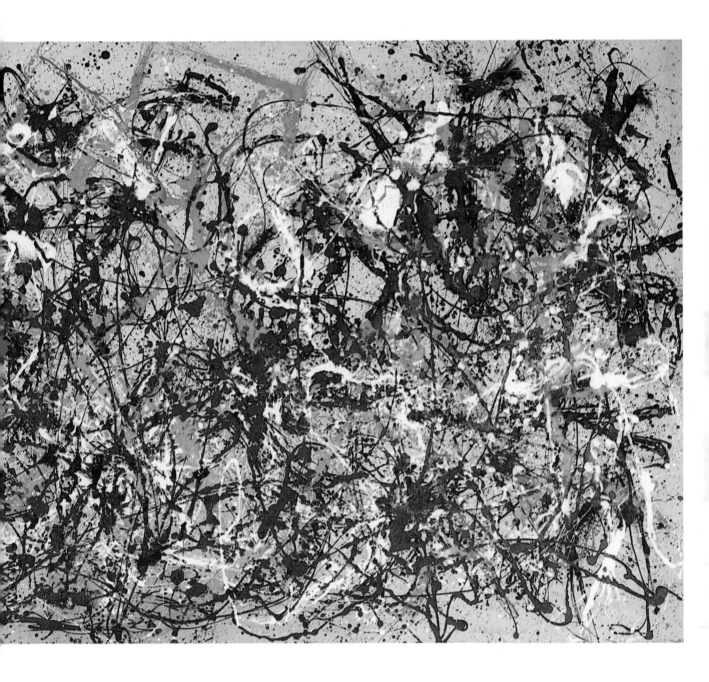

Autumn Rhythm, by Jackson Pollock. 1950.
Oil on canvas, 105 x 207 inches.
The Metropolitan Museum of Art, New York, New York.
George A. Hearn Fund, 1957.
Photograph © 1980, The Metropolitan Museum of Art.
© 1994 The Pollock-Krasner Foundation/ARS, New York.

Mural, by Jackson Pollock. 1943. Oil on canvas, 238 x 97¼ inches.
The University of Iowa Museum of Art, Iowa City, Iowa. Gift of Peggy Guggenheim.
© 1994 The Pollock-Krasner Foundation/ARS, New York.

Jackson Pollock wanted people to
feel and see the energy he felt while
painting. Even though you can't

recognize any objects in Jackson's most famous paintings, they are filled with expression, movement, and rhythm.

While Jackson was growing up, his
family moved all over the western
states, usually from one ranch or farm
to another. No matter how much work
needed to be done, Mrs. Pollock always

preferred to see her sons working on anything having to do with art. It was probably because of her encouragement that two of Jackson's older brothers also became artists.

When Jackson was eight years
old, his family moved to Janesville,
California. Many Native Americans
lived in the area. Sometimes Jackson
and his brothers would sneak up into
the mountains to the Native American
burial grounds and watch their
ceremonial dances.

Bird,
by Jackson
Pollock. 1941.
Oil and sand
on canvas,
27 3/4 x 24 1/4
inches.
The Museum of
Modern Art,
New York. Gift
of Lee Krasner
in memory of
Jackson Pollock.
© 1994 The
Pollock-Krasner
Foundation/ARS,
New York.
Photograph
© 1993 The
Museum of
Modern Art,
New York.

A Native American woman who helped take care of Jackson and his brothers often told them Native American legends. Years later, Jackson put mythological Native American creatures and symbols into some of his paintings.

When Jackson Pollock was just beginning high school in California, his oldest brother, Charles, was studying to be an artist in New York City. Charles often sent Jackson art magazines and wrote him letters about what he was learning. Jackson always admired his older brother's talent.

When Jackson was eighteen, his brother Charles returned home for a visit. When it was time for Charles to

return to New York, Jackson went
with him. He had decided to become
a serious artist, too.

When Jackson got to New York,
he entered the same art school that
Charles was going to, and had the
same teacher, Thomas Hart Benton.

Arts of the West, by Thomas Hart Benton. 1932.
Tempera with oil glaze, 96 x 156 inches.
New Britain Museum of American Art, Connecticut.
Harriet Russell Stanley Fund.

Thomas Hart Benton was already a famous American artist at that time. He was known for his large murals. A mural is a huge painting made to cover a wall or ceiling of a building. Jackson assisted Thomas Benton on some of his murals by posing, mixing paints, and cleaning the studio.

Jackson learned how large paintings were made, and tried to make his paintings look like Thomas Benton's. But Jackson had a difficult time giving his paintings the feeling and finished look he thought Thomas Benton would like.

Jackson Pollock always seemed to have trouble drawing things, too. No matter how hard he tried to make his drawings look the way he wanted, he just couldn't. It was almost like his hand and pencil refused to do what he wanted them to do.

Self Portrait, by Jackson Pollock. 1930. Oil on gesso ground on canvas, mounted on composition board, 7 1/4 x 5 1/4 inches. Courtesy Jason McCoy, Inc. © 1994 The Pollock-Krasner Foundation/ARS, New York.

Jackson often became angry and upset, but teachers kept working with him, because they knew how much he wanted to be an artist. The dark, gloomy look Jackson gave himself in the painting above might show how frustrated he felt.

One day, Jackson joined the workshop of a famous Mexican mural painter. David Siqueiros and his friends were experimenting with new types of paint and different ways of painting. They mixed oil colors with paint used for cars. They poured their colorful mixtures onto large canvases and spray-painted different surfaces just to see what would happen. Jackson was surprised. He noticed that beautiful and interesting shapes were being created.

Jackson thought that what he was
learning at Siqueiros' workshop might
help him create his own artwork
without having to draw perfectly.

During this time, Jackson learned all he could from the artwork of other modern artists whose paintings were shown at museums and galleries all over New York.

Jackson loved the mysterious, frightening, dreamlike scenes José Orozco painted in his murals. The strong, powerful shapes and symbols Pablo Picasso used reminded Jackson of Native American art, and brought back memories from his past.

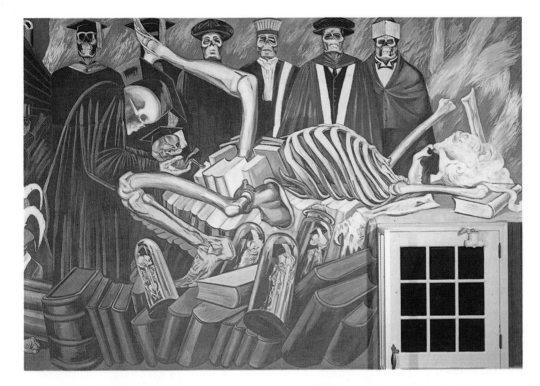

The Epic of American Civilization, Panel #17: *Gods of the Modern World,* by José Clemente Orozco. 1932-34. Fresco. Commissioned by the Trustees of Dartmouth College, Hanover, New Hampshire.

Guernica, by Pablo Picasso. Oil on canvas, 128 x 308 inches.
Museo Reina Sofia, Madrid, Spain.
Giraudon / Art Resource, New York.
©1994 ARS, New York / SPADEM, Paris, France.

Male and Female,
by Jackson Pollock.
1942. Oil on canvas,
73 x 49 inches.
Philadelphia
Museum of Art,
Pennsylvania.
Gift of Mr. and Mrs.
H. Gates Lloyd.
© 1994 The
Pollock-Krasner
Foundation/ARS,
New York.

Stenographic Figure, by Jackson Pollock. 1942. Oil on linen, 40 x 56 inches.
The Museum of Modern Art, New York. Mr. and Mrs. Walter Bareiss Fund.
© 1994 The Pollock-Krasner Foundation/ARS, New York.
Photograph © 1993 The Museum of Modern Art, New York.

Jackson started to combine all the things he had learned with shapes and symbols from his own imagination. Soon his paintings started to look very different from anything he'd done before. He was finally developing his own way of painting, and people began to notice his brightly colored work.

Jackson kept using his imagination
and began to create paintings that
were *really* different. Symbols and
shapes started to disappear, and his

Blue Poles, by Jackson Pollock. 1952. Oil, enamel and aluminum paint, glass on canvas, 83 x 185 ⅝ inches. Collection of National Gallery of Australia, Canberra.
© 1994 The Pollock-Krasner Foundation/ARS, New York.

works became larger. He started to drip and splatter paint all over his canvas as a way to show his feelings.

In 1945, Jackson bought a
farmhouse and married his girlfriend,
Lee Krasner. Lee was an artist, too.
She used one of the bedrooms of their
house for a studio, and Jackson used
the barn.

Jackson usually tacked his canvas
to the barn floor. He liked to walk all
around and be *in* his painting while
he worked. This way, Jackson felt that
he was really part of his work.

Jackson Pollock died in a car accident in 1956 when he was only forty-four years old. Even though he became famous during his life, he was often very unhappy.

Night Sounds, by Jackson Pollock. 1944.
Oil and pastel on canvas, 43 x 46 inches. Private Collection.
© 1994 The Pollock-Krasner Foundation/ARS, New York.

White Light, by Jackson Pollock. 1954.
Oil, enamel, and aluminum paint on canvas,
48 ¼ x 38 ¼ inches.
The Museum of Modern Art, New York.
The Sidney and Harriet Janis Collection.
© 1994 The Pollock-Krasner Foundation/ARS, New York.
Photograph © 1993 The Museum of Modern Art, New York.

Important people from all over the world loved to talk and write and argue about his exciting new paintings, but hardly anyone bought his work until years later.

Sometimes people have trouble understanding Jackson Pollock's paintings. They feel that anyone could have thrown paint around and done just as good a job. But Jackson knew exactly what he was doing. When you stand in front of a huge Jackson Pollock painting, you can get a feeling of being surrounded by light and color, movement and energy, that is very exciting!

Number 13A: Arabesque, by Jackson Pollock. 1948.
Oil on canvas, 37 ¼ x 116 ½ inches.
Yale University Art Gallery, New Haven, Connecticut.
Lent by Richard Brown Baker.
© 1994 The Pollock-Krasner Foundation/ARS, New York.

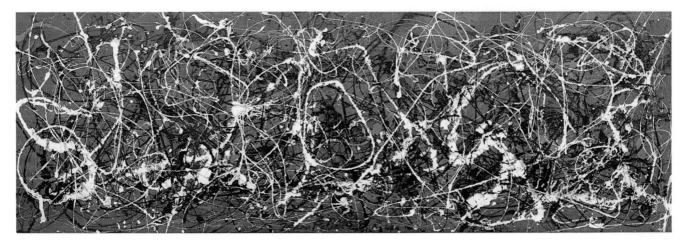

It's a good idea to see Jackson Pollock's paintings in person. The special feeling you get of being in an explosion of color and energy has a lot to do with their large size. The metallic and other different types of paint Jackson used help add to that feeling, too.

Detail of *Composition with Pouring II*

The paintings in this book came from

Baker Library, Dartmouth College, Hanover, New Hampshire

Hirshhorn Museum and Sculpture Garden, Smithsonian Institution, Washington, D.C.

Joslyn Art Museum, Omaha, Nebraska

The Metropolitan Museum of Art, New York, New York

Museo Reina Sofia, Madrid, Spain

The Museum of Modern Art, New York, New York

National Gallery of Australia, Canberra, Australia

New Britain Museum of American Art, New Britain, Connecticut

Philadelphia Museum of Art, Philadelphia, Pennsylvania

Smithsonian American Art Museum, Washington, D.C.

The University of Iowa Museum of Art, Iowa City, Iowa

Yale University Art Gallery, New Haven, Connecticut

LEARN MORE BY TAKING THE
POLLOCK QUIZ!

(ANSWERS ON THE NEXT PAGE.)

1. When Jackson was a young boy, he lost the tip of his pointer finger. How did this happen?

a. A friend accidentally cut it off when the boys were chopping wood.

b. While on a camping trip, Jackson lost his finger fighting off an angry badger.

c. It was bitten off while he was hand-feeding his pet piranha.

2. Jackson Pollock's painting style is known as Abstract Expressionism or Action Painting. What is another term is used to describe his style?

a. Splatter Painting

b. Drip Painting

c. Who is Responsible for this Mess Painting

3. Aside from paint, what other things might you find on or in a Jackson Pollock painting?

a. Carpet tacks, sand, tobacco, and bits of broken glass

b. Pizza crust, soda bottle caps, and torn-up electric bills

c. Banana peels, fingernail clippings, and ants

4. Before becoming an artist, what were some other jobs Jackson had?

a. He worked on a surveying crew

b. He was a school janitor

c. He was a lumberjack

d. All of the above

5. TRUE OR FALSE: Before becoming a painter, Jackson Pollock was more interested in being a sculptor.

ANSWERS

1. a Even though he made up all kinds of exciting stories about the way he lost his finger, the truth was that four-year-old Jackson lost it by accident when his friend chopped it off. Fortunately for Jackson, it never interfered with his ability to paint.

2. b Because Jackson's paintings were so new and different, art historians and writers had to come up with a name to describe his work. Today, Abstract Expressionism, Action Painting and Drip Painting are used to describe the work of Jackson and other artists of the time.

3. a For his totally new modern paintings, Jackson felt it was important to get away from the usual way artists had been painting. He preferred to use sticks, turkey basters, dried brushes, and trowels to drip and splatter paint onto his canvas.

Adding sand, broken glass and other weird things to his paintings was all part of his new style and look.

4. d Jackson had lots of different job experiences while he was growing up. Some of them, especially those in the outdoor wilderness, brought him closer to nature. Capturing a feeling of nature's light and energy was an important feature Jackson wanted to get across in his paintings.

5. TRUE As a young artist, Jackson liked sculpting better than painting. After working on sculptures for a while, Jackson found chipping away at stone was way too slow a process. Jackson had so many ideas and changed his mind so quickly, he found it much easier to express himself using paint on canvas.